The Art

of

Manifestation

By
Issachar Bey

"All life is a manifestation of the spirit, the manifestation of love."
– Morihei Ueshiba

Table of Contents

In Loving Memory

Joseph Sayles

Blas Avena

This Book is Dedicated to:

Joel Kulander
Neil Moffit
Patrick Morrison
Matt Galligan
Daron Wagner
Malley Rosen
Carlos Lossa
Gaz Brooks
Karen Anderson
Sal wise
Elaine Anne
Robert Morgan
Jason Hennessey
Shane Lockhart
Camell Page
Patrick Akau
Boomer
Kristyn Konia
Ryan Crohn
Brian Moore
Megan La Duke

Zoran Kizo
Daron Garrett

Ken Peters
AC Reed
Nalei Beazley
Orlando Okuendo
Kevin Ramaz
Rich Kenny
Micah Kia
Taylor Tamburo
Matt Roman
Tony Sciame
Gabe Fong
Rob Del Pozo
Adam Frescas
Shonda Hopkins
Keith Mathis
Erika Reynada
Joe Rytel
Jason McCoy
Jesse Arellano
Greg Baker
Anthony
Rodriguez
Kim Schioldan
Qasim Muhammad

Marcus Bryant
David Wagner
Ray Davila
Joe Santiago
Carlos Harper
Adam McClain
Lauren Hanley
Robby Reyes
Isaiah Gonzalez
Ken Donovan
Lloyd Garcia
Angie Feliciano
De'Vaughn Furch
Joseph Brooks
Dylan Close
Noah Wolcott
Urian Booze
Allen Diego
Dre Dismond
James Carrington
John Hernandez

Chapter 1
Your Thoughts Become Your Reality

"Thought is a force - a manifestation of energy – having a magnet-like power of attraction."
- William Walker Atkinson

Thought is the only reality; conditions are but its outward manifestations. As your thought changes, all outward or material conditions must change in order to be in harmony with their creator, which is thought.

Therefore, never forget that by default thoughts become things! Your reality is purely a manifestation of what you believe and think inside the deepest layers of your mind. Even at this moment, with each thought that is germinating inside your mind, you are planting a seed of manifestation which is going to affect your physical reality sooner or later.
It is important to understand that everything in this Universe is made of energy.

The process of creation always begins with a thought or an idea. If today we have a light bulb, it is because Thomas Edison had once gotten the thought to create it. Thoughts are indeed powerful energetic vibrations that are constantly spinning the wheels of creation. Now, you might argue that you constantly think about becoming rich, but in your reality you are loaded with debt? The answer is simple, look closely at the workings of your mind. You are most likely not thinking and feeling what it is like to be rich. Rather you are constantly thinking about your monetary problems and lack of funds.

The Conscious, The Subconscious and The Unconscious

Here, it becomes important to understand the different parts of the mind. The mind can be divided into three parts: the conscious, the subconscious and the unconscious. The conscious mind is like the tip of the iceberg with thoughts stemming from our current awareness. For example, your awareness about the book you are reading right now or the chair you are sitting on at this moment.

The subconscious mind, on the other hand, is a storehouse of accessible information. This is where the programming of your brain takes place. For example, when you were learning to drive, you were mostly using your conscious mind. But now when you can drive without giving much thought to it, it's because the subconscious has become programmed to do so.

The third part of the mind, the unconscious, is a storehouse of mostly inaccessible information along with our most primitive instincts and drives.

The Subconscious and the Manifestation of Our Reality

It is not what we think using our conscious mind that becomes our reality, but instead it is the programming of our subconscious that forges our Reality!

The reason why what we consciously think we want does not manifest into reality is because we have allowed ourselves to become programmed to constantly think about all that we don't want. So if you want to become rich then you must reprogram your subconscious mind to think only about what it is like to be rich and not about getting out of debt or to 'not be poor.' In order for your desire to manifest you must feel that you are already rich and are enjoying the things that you want to have.

Aligning your feelings with your thoughts is the key to creating what you desire in physical reality!

Cause and Effect

You must constantly monitor your thoughts because every thought is a cause and every corresponding condition is its effect. For this reason, it is essential that you control your thoughts to bring forth your desired conditions.

Ask yourself, are you thinking about what you want or are you engaged in thinking fearful thoughts about all the things you don't want. To create your desired reality, you must allow yourself to vibrate with the energy of love and gratitude which means that you must think happy thoughts about how good it is to have already received what you want.

The thumb rule for thoughts becoming things is simple: you receive what you feel and think about. Emotions play a very important role in manifestation because emotions are the fertilizer that enriches the soils of creation inside your mind.

What you think about with all your emotions is bound to become your Reality. So if you are thinking about what might go wrong or what has gone wrong, then you are aligning yourself with the emotion of fear. With every thought you thinking in this direction, you are creating a reality with more of what you DON'T want. To bring about a positive change in your life, you must feel the emotions of trust and gratitude that you have already received what you are asking for.

The saying goes, seek and it shall be given!

Manifestation and the Law of Attraction

Thoughts manifest through what is called **The Law of Attraction** which is based upon the principle of like attracts like or, in other words, as a Man thinketh, so shall he and his life become!

If you are thinking negative thoughts, then you are attracting negative things, circumstances, and people into your life. On the other hand, if you are thinking positive thoughts, then you are attracting positive things, circumstances, and people into your life. This is a law that works each time every time and there are no exceptions to it!

So now the question is what if currently your bills are piled high, your partner has left you or your boss has informed you about your ensuing layoff? Are you responsible for all this mess? Well, the answer is an absolute YES!

I know that's not pleasant to hear. However, the good news is that just like you have created all these undesirable things with your negative thinking and feeling, you can also create what you actually want to experience using the Law of

Remember, even at this moment, your thoughts are creating your reality. A thought is very much like a boomerang. It goes out into the universe and ALWAYS comes back to you in the experience of your life. The type of thought you are thinking determines exactly what is coming back to you. If you are thinking about the good things you want, then it is bringing those back to you. However, if you are thinking about all the disastrous things that can happen, then that is exactly what you are receiving.

Self-Analysis and reflection

It's time you reviewed your thoughts and emotions. What are you thinking about right now? How are you feeling? What is it that you want? What are your desires?

Write these down to create a clear mental picture of exactly what you want to experience in your life and in your reality.

Change your thoughts, change your life

"A thought is a Cosmic Order waiting to happen."

- Stephen Richards

The formula for change is simple: Transform your thoughts and you can transform your life. Years of fearful conditioning has programmed us to think of the worst under all circumstances. Have you ever noticed that you automatically think the worst in some or most situations?

Like when you go to the doctor and have a test done. Don't you normally have to fight hard to counter the negative thoughts that seem to automatically emerge? It's almost like the brain has gotten hard wired towards thinking negative like the brain has gotten hard wired towards thinking negative so now it is very important to learn how to re-train your mind to think positive under all circumstances because, like we said earlier, with every thought you are shaping your current and future reality!

Easier said than done, isn't it? But here's how you can reclaim your power and your life back through a strategic step-by-step approach:

- **Monitor your thought life**

  Make a commitment to monitor your thoughts for 30 days. Observe what types of thoughts are running in your mind. Are they positive or negative? Take note of the negative thoughts that come by writing down the predominant ones.

- **Transform negative thoughts into positive ones**

  Pick your negative thoughts and turn them into positive ones. For example, if you tend to think this a lot of "I never seem to get ahead", I want you to write that down and then strike it out. Now, in its place, write a positive statement to counteract the previous statement:

  "I am constantly making significant progress and improvement in everything I do."

- **Speak your thoughts out aloud**

  Every time a negative thought occurs, pause for a moment and counteract it by saying out aloud a positive statement. Obviously, if you are surrounded by people, then you can just say it aloud inside your mind.

Here's an example, if you catch yourself thinking about car accidents and the possibility of something like that happening to you, stop yourself and say out aloud, "I travel safely. Only good things happen to me."

Never forget that repetition is the key to retraining your mind. Repetition inscribes a new positive thought into the deep recesses of the subconscious mind from which all our repetitive thoughts and habits emerge.

It is also advisable to make a list of positive affirmations relevant to you and read them out aloud every day as many times as you can. By doing so, you are not only re-wiring your brain, but your positive thoughts are also actually going out into the universe attracting positive situations and circumstances into your life.

If you can continue this observation for 30 days, then you would have formed a new habit in which thinking positive will begin to come naturally!

Let go of the past and Let in What You Want!!

Who you are and what your life is like today is a reflection of all the thoughts you have had in the past and are most likely thinking even now. Knowing and acknowledging this right now is a tremendously empowering thing to do because this is your chance to reclaim your power as the creator of your life story. This is your chance to manifest the abundant and joyful life you have always dreamt of having. And it all begins with a positive thought in the right direction!

You really are what you think, so think awesome, think positive!

Clear Mental Picture of What You Want & The Power of Imagination

The power of imagination has been under-rated. Often dismissed as day-dreaming or wishful thinking, imagination is in truth the key that opens the door of manifestation and abundance. When you experience in your imagination what you wish to experience in your reality, you allow yourself to feel the same emotions as you would feel if your desire was already part of your present reality.

By doing this, you are aligning yourself fully with the energy of your desires. This sends a clear and powerful message into the Universe that you are ready to receive what you are asking for and like a faithful servant, the universe always delivers exactly what you are asking for each time and every time!

However, it is very important to have a crystal clear image of exactly what you want. If you want a new car, then you must visualize the car in its minutest detail. What is its color, is it a sedan or a hatchback, how many doors does it have, how fast can you drive it and so on. The clearer the picture you have inside your mind, the more likely you are to receive exactly what you are asking for.

Action Strategy

On a sheet of paper, write down the answers to the following questions as clearly and concretely as possible.

Questions to Ask Yourself

1. What is the purpose of your life?
2. What are the things you need to do to fulfill your life's purpose?
3. What are the things that make you feel fulfilled?
4. What gifts and talents do you possess?
5. What do you think is your ideal vocation?
6. Do you want to turn what you love doing into a paid vocation? How can you do this?

Things to Keep in Mind

7. Have a crystal clear picture of exactly what you want to manifest.
8. Write down all the things you can do to manifest your desire.
9. Research and learn as much as you can about the things you want to manifest.
10. See yourself in your Mind's Eye doing, having, and being all that you want to manifest.
11. Replace all negative thoughts with new positive ones

12. Surround yourself with people who make you feel loved and confident. Lovingly distance yourself from people who have a negative outlook towards life and towards others.

Affirmation

"I am now walking on my true Life Path with definite, concrete steps.
The doors of success, happiness and fulfillment are opening all around me as I keep moving forward with joyful thoughts and a happy heart.
I am now attracting and rejoicing in an endless supply of abundance, happiness and fulfillment."

Notes

_____

_____

_____

_____

_____

_____

_____

_____

_____

_____

_____

_____

_____

_____

_____

_____

_____

_____

_____

Notes

Chapter 2
Unleashing the Power of Happiness!

"It's really important that you feel good. Because this feeling good is what goes out as a signal into the universe and starts to attract more of itself to you. So the more you can feel good, the more you will attract the things that help you feel good and that will keep bringing you up higher and higher."
– Joe Vitale

Have you ever wondered why you want to manifest that pay hike or your soul mate or that new car? What is the guiding force that makes you desire all these things? The answer at the end is always going to be the same: happiness. Isn't it?

If you will receive the pay hike; you will be happy, if you will find your soul mate, you will be happy; if you will acquire that new car, you will be happy. In essence, everything we want or desire is because we believe it will make us happy.

Now, the problem is that we treat these circumstances as the cause and the resulting happiness as its effect when in truth happiness is our very nature and our birthright that needs no external factors to flourish inside our hearts. Just look at a baby, does he need any external stimulant to be happy. He is blissful and content with everything he has. External factors might add to his happiness from time to time, but they definitely can't define it for him. You were also once that baby who needed no external reason to be happy because happiness was and still is your very nature.

It is time to reclaim your true Self; that inner child who is always blissful and content because it is that happy child who has the power to spin the wheels of manifestation in his or her favor!!

You must be wondering what on earth this last statement actually means, aren't you? Please understand that our physical reality always corresponds with our mental and emotional state. If you are sad and bitter about how bad your life is, then you are constantly attracting situations and people who reflect this belief. On the other hand, if you are happy and believe that your life is full of miracles, then you are attracting miracles into your life.

Keeping a check on your emotional state is crucial for transforming your reality into what you want it to be. Easier said than done, I know! When something bad happens, like a terrible break-up or getting fired from a job or even someone hurling abuses at us, our emotional makeup automatically turns extremely negative.

The urge to sulk and writhe in self-pity becomes very strong and it is hard to break the vicious cycle of suffering we get sucked into. The problem is that the more we give into sulking and cursing the present situation and the people involved in it, the more negativity we are manifesting in our lives.

Believe it or not, you are 100% responsible for everything that is happening to you right now. If you want to change your life then you must accept this Truth. You would wonder how on earth you could have attracted a break-up with your partner whom you love so much, but if you will look closely then you will realize that there was most likely a deep-seated fear or insecurity involved on your part that caused the break-up in the first place.

Remember, it is not what you think consciously that becomes your reality, but the real emotions you feel along with the thoughts emerging from your subconscious mind that become your experience of life.

So for example, you want to trust your partner and you keep saying that you trust him or her very much, but there is an almost uncontrollable instinct making you want to hunt for sings of cheating like rummaging their phone for messages sent to someone else when they are not around, or, if you find them conversing with an attractive person of the opposite sex in a social setting, then you immediately begin wondering if they are interested in them.

So even though you think you trust your partner, your subconscious mind does not agree with you and your emotions are definitely not in alignment with the thought that you trust your partner.

What are you manifesting in this case: a happy loyal relationship or a relationship where you ultimately find out that your partner has been cheating on you? It is most likely going to be the latter because our thoughts and emotions by default attract people and create circumstances that we are genuinely expecting to experience.

Therefore, your subconscious thought patterns and emotions are powerful indicators of what you are truly expecting to experience. You must watch them carefully!

But the bigger question is; how can this pattern of negative thinking and manifestation be broken so that you can consciously attract all the things you truly want to experience?

The answer is simple; in order to change your reality, you must change your thoughts as we discussed in the previous chapter but along with making positive thinking a habit, you must also begin to FEEL HAPPY IN THE NOW!!

Remember, every time we react negatively towards a situation or person, it registers as a negative impression inside our subconscious mind. This becomes the cause of attracting more misery and misfortune into our lives.

Your reality begins to shift towards the positive, the moment you make a conscious effort to change your thoughts while aligning yourself with the emotion of happiness. Thus, you must feel happy in the NOW in order to create the future of your choice!

But the question is exactly how can you make yourself feel happy when everything seems to be going wrong in your life? Well, it's true that this is going to require some effort, but changing your emotions and your thoughts is crucial if you really want to change your life. Understand that nothing is permanent, no heartbreak, no loss, no run of bad luck. The wheels of fortune are going to turn again and you have the power to turn them in your favor.

Never forget that if you have unwittingly created negative things, then you also have the power to create the present and future of your choice. By feeling happy from NOW on, you are going to turn the wheels of fortune in your favor because YOU ARE THE CREATOR OF YOUR DESTINY!

So here's more on how to feel happy when things are going wrong. Under such circumstances, it is a good idea to disconnect yourself from the drama that surrounds you in order to connect with that which you really want.

For example, if you are in the middle of a debt crisis with no idea how you are going to pay it all back then you have to start visualizing that you are financially well-off and feel the emotions that go with it. Here, it is important to remember that NEVER feel that you are coming out of debt or that your debt problems are getting solved. This is because the Universe does not understand such statements where you are saying you DON'T want a problem. The Universe only understands that you are repeating 'debt problems' and that is what will be sent to you.

It is important to feel something fully positive in order to manifest something completely positive. And in this case, what is fully positive is visualizing that you are financially well off and that you are enjoying having all the things you want. Make the picture inside your mind as concrete as possible: see yourself living in your dream house, driving your dream car, taking holidays to your favorite destinations, etc.

The thing is that the mind does not understand the difference between 'real' and 'imagined' events; it is going to produce the same emotional response in either case. And emotions along with positive thoughts are what you need in order to fully change your circumstances!

Happiness and the Science of Energetic Frequency

Have you ever wondered why some people seem to rub you the wrong way even without even speaking a word to you? Talking about the other extreme, have you ever wondered why sometimes there is an instant connection with someone and time seems to fly when you are with them? It is all because everything in this world is energy; including you and your thoughts. When we are around people who have a similar energetic frequency to ours, there is a peaceful and harmonious association.

On the other hand, there is an instant sense of repulsion when there is a strong mismatch of energetic frequency.

Similarly, our thoughts also have energetic frequencies. Negative thoughts vibrate at a very low frequency and therefore attract negative circumstances and people to us who are also vibrating at a lower frequency.

When we are happy and thinking joyful thoughts, we are vibrating at a higher frequency and therefore attracting experiences and people who are also vibrating at a higher frequency. So if you are wondering why your desire hasn't manifested yet, it is most likely because your energetic frequency is not matching with the energetic frequency of your desire.

In order to align yourself with the energetic frequency of your desire, you must change your thoughts and emotions to those vibrating at a higher frequency. And for that the

easiest thing you can do right now is to simply allow yourself to FEEL GOOD!!

Remember, there is always something to be grateful for, something to enjoy and something to relish no matter how grim you think your situation is. It helps to keep a gratitude journal. Make it a habit to write down every day at least 10 things that you are grateful for. Read it several times every day especially when faced with challenging circumstances.

Another thing you must do is constantly think about your desired outcome as if it has already happened and feel happy about it. For example, if you want a new car, then you have to feel like you are sitting in the driver's seat with the steering wheel in your hands maneuvering the car along your favorite driveways in town. Don't worry about how it is all going to materialize. The "how's" are the department of the Universe to figure out!

Once you have aligned yourself fully with the energetic frequency of the outcome you desire, the Universe will find a way of making it happen for you. You have to trust and you have to stay positive by keeping yourself aligned with the energetic frequency of your desired outcome at all times. This is certainly not going to be very easy but it is the only way you can make your life what you want it to be.

Don't worry, be happy

Remember the catchy song "Don't worry, be happy"?
The lyrics go:

"In every life we have some trouble.
When you worry you make it double
Don't worry, be happy
Don't worry, be happy now."

Seems like the writer of this song understood a bit about the Law of Attraction as he is quite right in saying, "When you worry you make it double."

Your feelings in the NOW are what matter. Your feelings in the NOW are determining what your future is going to be. As tempting as it is to stay sad, angry, or frustrated, DON'T do it!! If you will give in now, then you will have to deal with more undesirables in the future.

So feel happy NOW. Sing a song. Dance a fun dance. Laugh out loud. Make a joke. Giggle at life.

After all, it's only one life you got!!

Action Strategy

1. Stay positive and happy no matter what your current circumstances are because your thoughts and emotions in the NOW are creating your future.

2. Do not ponder about your problems lest you will manifest more of those.

3. Constantly keep yourself aligned with the energetic frequency of the outcome you desire by imagining and feeling that it has already happened.

4. Do not doubt or worry about how it is all going to come about. When you trust that the Universe has already fulfilled your desire, then all channels of creation and manifestation will open up. Miracles will happen! Just believe.

5. Maintain a gratitude journal. Every single day, write down at least 10 things you are grateful for and read it several times throughout the day.

6. Grab a lunch date with your friend, book yourself for a massage session, take a hobby class, do things that make you happy!!

Affirmation

"I am peaceful, I am joyful; I am happy.
All expected and unexpected doors of manifestation have opened up attracting to me my heart's desire.
Right at this moment, I am living an abundant fulfilling life with all my dreams having come true."

Notes

_____

_____

_____

_____

_____

_____

_____

_____

_____

_____

_____

_____

_____

_____

_____

_____

_____

_____

_____

_____

Notes

_____

_____

_____

_____

_____

_____

_____

_____

_____

_____

_____

_____

_____

_____

_____

_____

_____

_____

_____

_____

Chapter 3
Your Goals and the Need to Write Them Down

"Successful people maintain a positive focus in life no matter what is going on around them. They stay focused on their past successes rather than their past failures, and on the next action steps they need to take to get them closer to the fulfillment of their goals rather than all the other distractions that life presents to them." - Jack Canfield

You can't have what you want until you know exactly what it is you want! And then, once you know what you want you must also write it down. Why? Well, let us explore the answer to this in depth as it is one of the most important things you are going to be doing to turn your dreams into reality.

Scientific Evidence Proving the Importance of Writing Down Goals

A study done in 1979 at Harvard University has illustrated just how important clearly writing down your goals and an action plan for achieving them is. In this study, graduates from the college were asked if they had taken the time to write down their life goals and if they have a plan in place for pursuing them. Here's what was found:

- 3% had written down detailed goals and had a solid action plan in place.
- 13% said they had goals, but had not written them down.
- 84% said they had no concrete goals at all.

Ten years later a follow-up study was compiled and it was reported that the 3% who had written goals down were 10 times more successful than the rest 97%. This study is a significant indicator that having clear-cut goals, writing them down and having a solid action plan in place for pursuing them is very important for success!!

It's Never Too Late

I hear many people talk about their desires and dreams, but they simply don't take the steps for turning them into reality. And then, I also hear from people how they have given up on their most cherished dreams because at some point, they simply stopped believing that it was possible to reach their goals and now have resorted to living a sad, miserable life feeling like a victim.

The good news is that no matter how late you think you are in the game now, there is still time. Yes, you can still resurrect your goals and create your dream life. Today is always a new day and it NEVER is too late to go after your heart's desire!!!

Jet-set GOAL

Have you ever seen an architect work? He creates a blueprint and then turns it into physical reality with hard work, determination and persistence. You are the architect of your destiny, but you can't create your dream life until you have a blueprint for it!

By setting a goal and having an action plan in place for pursuing it, you are adding fuel to the jetliner of your dreams that is ready to be launched into the infinite skies of success!

And when you start living 'as if' it has all already happened, then you align yourself fully with the energetic reality of your goals. If you can do this, then nothing can stop you from attaining full-blown success. Trust me, just about nothing can stop you from winning this game of life!

So let's get back to goal setting now. Here's how to set short and long-term goals:

Define Your Goals

How can you achieve something without knowing exactly what it is you want?

Hence, the first thing you must do for any kind of goal setting is to actually sit down and figure out what you want. Sure, you might know a lot about all that you don't want, but WHAT IS IT THAT YOU ACTUALLY WANT? You will most likely need some quality time by yourself to figure it all out. You don't want to rush through this step. Take a few days, a week or even a month to really contemplate what you want in both the short and the long-term.

Write Your Goals Down

Once you have taken the time to think about what you want in and out of life, write your goals down on two separate sheets of paper or make two separate Word document files on your computer; one for your Short-term goals and another one for your Long-term goals. Short-term goals will consist of goals that you want to accomplish within a short period of time; perhaps 3 to 6 months or less. Long-term goals consist of goals that might take you a year or more to accomplish.

Hang Your List of Goals at a Prominent Place

Reading your goals every day is the best way of internalizing them! Therefore, you would want to pin or hang up your list of goals at a prominent place. For example, your office wall, your refrigerator, your bedroom wall or just about any place that you visit every day and spend a considerable amount of time at can be a great place for reminding you of your goals. Remember, the more often you read or think about something, the deeper it sinks into your subconscious.

And why is that important? Simply because you are always more likely to act on thoughts and feelings emerging from your subconscious which makes you more likely to succeed in accomplishing your goals once the message for what you want to accomplish has reached your subconscious.

Call for Action and Energetic Alignment

Once you have your list of goals ready, you must form a realistic action plan. For instance, if you want a new job, then write down what action steps you will take every day towards finding one: Searching for and filling out suitable job applications, revamping your resume, networking, connecting with a job placement agency, etc.

Your actions send out a clear message into the Universe that you are working towards achieving what you want and the Universe will respond by bringing the right circumstances and people into your life which will help you in realizing your dreams.

The other extremely important thing is to always remain in perfect energetic alignment with your goals. You have to live as if you already have it all. This can certainly get very hard and challenging because it is hard for most of us to believe in something that we can't see with our physical eyes.

Trust that your goals have already materialized in energetic reality and they are on their way to getting delivered at your doorstep. When it gets hard to retain this faith then just ask yourself what emotions do you really want to feel: sadness and misery that your dreams are lost or happiness and joy (even if it is simulated) that what you want is already yours. The latter is certainly not easy but it does seem like a better deal, doesn't it?

Seek and it shall be given, trust and it shall be yours!!

Action Strategy

1. Do not underestimate the importance of writing your goals down.

2. Have two separate sheets or files for your Short-term and Long-term goals.

3. Have an action plan for accomplishing your goals and act on it.

4. Always remain in energetic alignment with your goals aka live as if it has all already happened.

Affirmation

"Right at this moment, I have accomplished all my goals.
My heart beats with joy and happy anticipation because I know that everything I want is already mine.
I trust that all that I wish for comes to me in perfect Divine Timing.
Indeed, truly blessed my life and I am."

Notes

Notes

Chapter 4
There Can Be No Manifestation
Without Action

*"When it is obvious that the goals cannot be reached, don't
adjust the goals, adjust the action steps."*
- *Confucius*

Setting your intentions straight and visualizing that
everything you want has already happened is the key for
manifesting your dreams. However, this is not the same as
being an idle day-dreamer.

While you continue to add fuel to the fire of your most
greatly cherished dreams by constantly thinking and feeling
as if all that you wish for has already transpired, you also
need to take direct action to set-forth and accelerate the
manifestation process. In fact, manifestation without action
is not possible!

Imagine you are a car whose dream is to arrive at a lovely
landscape several miles away from the madness of the city.
Now, in this case, your visualizations will be the fuel that will
fire the gas tank of your car, but your actions will be the four
tires of the car that will actually take you to your goals. You
can't arrive at your destination with a fired up gas tank
alone.

The Law of Attraction brings the right opportunities and
people to you but in order to attain success, you must ACT
on them!!

Why it sometimes seems like the Law of Attraction is not working?

Sometimes people give up too soon thinking that the Law of Attraction is not working. Despite constantly repeating positive affirmations and visualizations, it seems to them that the Law is not working. If you are experiencing something similar then please know that the Law of Attraction works each time and every time. All the powers of manifestation come into play once you clearly put forward your desire into the Universe along with the right emotional energy.

However, one reason why you might not have seen results yet could be because your approach is lacking a potent and powerful action plan.

Action Plan & The GVA Formula

So what really is a powerful action plan? A powerful action plan is a highly practical and doable plan of action that you create and implement in your life. We will talk more about this in the next chapter. But for now, please understand that your action plan sends a message into the Universe that you are taking steady and constant steps towards your goals and are ready to embrace your dreams at any moment.

For example, let's say you want to be a doctor. If you simply sit around thinking and visualizing that you already are a doctor performing surgery on a patient that doesn't mean you will become a doctor. There are certain steps you must take; like applying to medical school, studying for exams, applying for the right job, etc.

So we can say that goal setting and visualization without action is like a body without soul or vice versa. In order to get what you want, you must create a perfect combination of all three.

Let's call this the GVA formula of successful manifestation: Goal Setting, Visualization & Action.

Patience and Faith

Along with the GVA formula, you must also practice these two virtues of immense value: patience and faith.

Always remember that the road to get to your dreams is not an easy one; there can be delays and temporary setbacks. But don't give up, keep charging ahead and one day you will definitely arrive where you want to be.

Please understand that our dreams and goals do not always manifest within the time frames we assign to them. It is best to not impose any timelines. Let go of wanting to have control. Have patience and complete faith that what you want has already happened and it will only be a matter of time before you find out how right you are in believing so!

Also, understand that every moment you dedicate towards practicing the GVA formula for manifestation is shortening the distance between your present reality and your dreams. In fact, just believe that at this very moment there is no distance between your present and your dreams. It is all already here; waiting to be revealed in your physical reality at any moment.

Do not give up on your dreams and on the practice of the GVA formula if temporary setbacks come. Think of facing setbacks as similar to the process of trying to open a lock with a bunch of keys in which only one key is the right one. Just because you have tried twenty keys from the key chain and didn't open the lock doesn't mean that the twenty-first one isn't going to work either. In fact, the twenty-first key might be the one that actually opens the lock. Keep going and success has to be yours!!

Also, trust that everything is coming to you in perfect divine timing. It is all going to fall into place and when you will look back a while later, it will make perfect sense why everything happened the way it did. Enjoy the journey and the arrival will be even more fun.

The Toxic Habit of Procrastination

Nothing delays the manifestation process more than the vicious habit of procrastination. I call it 'vicious' because if you procrastinate today, then you will most likely procrastinate tomorrow as well, and then you will do the same the day after as well and so on.

Procrastination in the now builds a never-ending cycle of putting off the necessary actions for another time and the longer this continues the harder it gets to break the cycle.

Understand that procrastination stifles your growth and breaks your momentum. It's easy to put off today what you can do tomorrow, but that kind of thinking can soon turn into difficult to get rid of habit.

In fact, it is this kind of thinking that keeps people in the same scenarios for years. If you are broke now and have a tendency to procrastinate taking the right actions, chances are you will be broke one year down the road as well. Get past it; break your own barriers and limitations. Do not put off doing what you can do now by convincing yourself that you are waiting for the perfect opportunity when it will all "feel right". By procrastinating, you are only delaying the manifestation of your goals.

If you start now instead of tomorrow, then you will arrive where you want to be one day early!!

Keep Charging Ahead

As you apply the GVA formula along with the practice of patience and faith, know that what you are wishing for has already been granted to you. The Universe is a faithful servant that always brings to you what you are asking for. Delays and setbacks can be part of the journey, but if you haven't yet arrived where you want to be trust that your journey isn't over yet. Keep charging ahead, keep doing what you are doing, keep believing in what you want and it is soon going to be yours.

Remember, your life is what you make it. So never stop making it AWESOME!

Action Strategy

1. Have a potent and powerful action plan in place.

2. Practice the GVA formula at all times.

3. Always have patience and faith.

4. Cauterize the toxic habit of procrastination.

5. Understand that temporary setbacks and delays are minor bumps on your journey. Your journey isn't over until you have arrived where you want to be!

Affirmation

"I am grateful to be surrounded by the right people and perfect opportunities.
I am happy and joyous to have all that I want.
I am destined for success.
I am at peace knowing that everything I want is already mine."

Notes

Notes

Chapter 5
How to Create a Powerful Action Plan to Get Exactly What You Want

"Our goals can only be reached through a vehicle of a plan, in which we must fervently believe, and upon which we must vigorously act. There is no other route to success."
- Stephen A. Brennan

So now that we have talked about the importance of a powerful action plan, let's get down to business and learn the nitty-gritty of creating one exclusively for you!

Key Elements of a powerful action plan

- It is formed keeping in mind your individual lifestyle and personality
- Practical and doable
- Has something for you to do every day or as frequently as possible
- Makes you feel like with every action, you are shortening the distance between your current place in life and your goal
- Your action plan has to be realistic. It shouldn't be so overwhelming that you manage to act on it one day or for two days, but by the third day it becomes impossible to fit it in your daily life
- The only person who knows what the best plan of action for you is YOU!!

How to Create Your Action Plan

So here's how you are going to go about creating your powerful action plan that is going to move all the forces of the Universe in your favor!

Write Down Your Goals and Your Action Plan

As we have discussed earlier, it is absolutely crucial to write down both your goals and your action plan for achieving them to keep your mind one-pointed and focused on your goal.

So before we get started on discussing things further, make sure that you have a few sheets of paper and pen handy.

Long and Short-Term Goals

Do not just write down your biggest goals in life, but also break it down into smaller goals attainable within a shorter period of time.

For example, if your ultimate goal is to become a brain surgeon, then break down your journey to get there into several small goals. So in this case, your goals for this year and for the next couple of years can be: clearing pre-med, med school, performing at the top of your class in med school, internship, specialization in brain surgery, etc.

Please understand that the human brain likes milestones and it is easier to accomplish the journey of a thousand miles by setting goals to make it through per hundred miles or fifty miles.

If the goals you set for your mind are too overwhelming then it will paralyze your mind into non-action. Therefore, you must break down your BIG goals into smaller ones.

Step-by-step Action Plan

Your action plan must be clear-cut, well-defined and realistic. So let's say your long term goal is to become an accomplished author and one of your short term goals is to get yourself published in a local newspaper. Now, you must write down a step-by-step action plan for getting yourself published in a local newspaper. For this, you will have to evaluate where you think you stand with your current writing skills. So your action plan can include:

- taking creative writing classes
- establishing contact with published authors to learn more about this skill
- maintaining a daily journal
- writing an article every day or every two days
- reading at least two books per week
- sourcing contact lists of newspapers in your local area
- submitting several articles to the each newspaper agency
- Staying persistent with your efforts and continuing to submit your work to newspapers until you finally get published

This is only a sample action plan. You will have to modify everything depending upon your lifestyle, your skills and the goal you have in sight. Just remember to keep everything clear-cut and doable.

The Importance of Discipline and Perseverance

Staying focused and determined to attain your goals isn't easy. There will be days when you will want to sleep a little longer, there will be days when you will want to go out and have fun, there will be days when you will even wonder if it really is worth working as hard as you are working, and then there will be days when you will question whether what you want is ever going to happen or not.

Here, you must cling onto discipline. Wake up even when you don't want to, work even when your friends are out having fun, immerse yourself in action when doubts and questions assail your mind.

Trust that the Universe always brings to you what you are asking for even when it seems like what you want might never happen. It is happening and it has already happened. Live as if you already have what you want and keep acting on your plan of action.

The path of success is not an easy one. Failure and setbacks will most likely come, but you must persist and you must stay disciplined in following your action plan. Have faith and it is all going to work out for your best. It just has to be that way because the Universe is a faithful servant who says to you each time and every time, "your wish is my command."

Remember, runners in a race don't stop running when they see a hurdle. They muster all their strength and skill to jump over each hurdle to keep going until they arrive at the finishing line. You must persevere even in the face of difficulties and setbacks.

Surround Yourself with Positive Resources and People

If you want to be a musician, then would you not hang out with the best musicians in town? If you want to be a doctor, then won't it be a great idea to learn from the best doctors in your country?

Surround yourself with people from whom you know you have something to learn and who share your interests and passions. Do not waste time with idle talk or spend too much time with people who are aimless. If you want to be a winner then you must be surrounded by winners at all times.

And yes, you don't have to be with winners in person, you can always just invest in books and DVDs created by people you look up to. You can also participate in seminars and workshops to hone your skills.

I will end with a quote by Will Smith, "TALENT YOU HAVE NATURALLY. Skill is only developed by hours and hours and hours of beating on your craft."

Action Strategy

1. Evaluate your long and short-term goals

2. Break down your long-term goals into several short-term goals

3. Ask yourself where you currently stand vis-à-vis where you want to be

4. Form a realistic and doable step-by-step action plan to achieve each short term goal that will eventually take you to your long term goals

5. Persevere and stay disciplined even in the face of setbacks and disappointments

6. Surround yourself with positive and encouraging people

7. If you want to be a winner then you must learn from winners!

8. Invest in resources that will help you hone your skills: books, CDs, DVDs, seminars, workshops, classes, etc.

Affirmation

"Every day in every way I am taking sure and steady steps towards my goals.
I am surrounded by wonderful positive people who are encouraging and helping me in fulfilling my life's mission.
Everything I need to know and learn finds a way of coming to me in perfect Divine Timing."

Notes

Notes

Chapter 6
Manifestation and the Vision Board

"If one advances confidently in the direction of his dreams, and endeavors to live the life which he has imagined, he will meet with a success unexpected in common hours. He will put some things behind, will pass an invisible boundary; new, universal, and more liberal laws will begin to establish themselves around and within him; or the old laws will be expanded, and interpreted in his favor in a more liberal sense, and he will live with the license of a higher order of beings." - Thoreau

When you see it, you get it

When it comes to manifesting what you want in your life, the power of visualization comes to be of immense value. By visualizing what you want with acute clarity and with all your emotions, you are sending a clear message into the Universe that you are ready to receive whatever it is you are asking for.

Some of the most successful men and women will tell you that they owe a major part of their success to clear goal setting and constant visualization. Actors daydream about being on stage acting, singers fantasize about giving their best performance in front of a crowd, professional football players close their eyes and see themselves scoring a touchdown and so on.

Never forget, what you seek is always (by default) what you receive!

How Long does it Take?

Now, one question I often get asked is exactly how long will it take for goals to manifest? Here, you must understand that time is an illusion. The Universe is Infinite and its potential is also infinite. In truth, the past, present and future are all happening simultaneously. You have to only look at the workings of your own mind to realize this truth. Tell me can't you see your past, present and future at the same time within your minds' eye?

Therefore, when you visualize what you want, you are always advised to do so as if it was happening right now. You don't visualize that you "will receive" what you want in the future otherwise you will keep yourself confined to the energetic reality of "will receive."

Anyway, coming back to the question, exactly how long will it actually take for your desires to fully manifest in physical reality? You have to understand that the limitation is inside your mind. More often than not, we unwittingly assign timelines to the manifestation of our desires and that is what delays their fulfillment. For instance, while desiring something Big, we think that it can't possibly manifest within a day or two.

Make a conscious effort to live as if everything you are wishing for is already there. Do not ask or doubt "when" it is going to happen, and you will be surprised by how soon the Universe will prove you right.

Maybe, you will meet a guy in the taxi you take to work who will offer you your dream job that also doubles your salary or perhaps some long lost relative will suddenly realize that he or she wants to gift his/her rather new Mercedes to you. The thing is you never know just how the Universe will make everything fall into place for you but it sure will fulfill your desires! The key is to set your intentions and then release all your worries about exactly how it is going to happen.

However, after you have set your intentions, you must also create an action plan. By following the action plan, you are taking concrete steps in the direction of your dreams. Visualization is crucial but working hard to achieve what you want is also equally important.

For instance, if you want to increase the turnover of your company by $100,000 then visualization will help clear the path of success for you but if you won't put in the hard work that is required to make your company grow then it will most likely not bring about the desired results. The Universe will support you when you will support yourself fully and you have to put in the hard work for that!

Vision Board

Another way in which you can expedite the manifestation process is by creating a Vision Board!!

So now, what exactly is a Vision Board?

A vision board is simply a board that one creates with a variety of visual stimulus in the form of images, words, and other triggers that represent one's goals and dreams. Your vision board acts as a concrete representation of the fulfillment of your most cherished goals and dreams.

It helps you add a strong element of Reality to the manifestation process because it is easier to believe in that which you can see in front of your eyes. Also, whenever your mind becomes assailed with doubts and fears, the vision board gently helps in bringing it back to the present so that you can regain focus on the manifestation process.

How to Create a Vision Board?

So here's how you can create your very own vision board:

Write Down All Your Goals and Dreams

You must write down with extreme clarity what your goals are in all the different spheres of life: health, relationships, work, social status, spirituality, etc.

Write down what you want in each of these areas as specifically as you can. For instance, if you want to become the managing director of your company, then you must write down "I am the managing director of my company earning $_____."

Remember, the more exact you are in what you want, the more likely you are to receive exactly what you are asking for. Also, there is no such thing as a 'selfish' goal or goals that are too small. Any legitimate desire that you have is worth finding its fulfillment. For example, if your desire is to own that red colored Dior dress, then write that down as well. Think about everything you want – sum up all your big and small dreams. Is it that sports car you desire or an exotic vacation to India, or a pair of Jimmy Choo shoes? Just write everything down.

You are a child of the Infinite Universe and it is your right to enjoy everything your heart craves!

Gather the materials

Things you need:
A nice poster board
Assorted magazines
Scissors
Glue/Tape

Dig into a huge stack of assorted magazines. Surround yourself with just about any magazine you can lay hands on. You never know what you might find in there. Once you have your resources ready, cut out images, words, quotes just about anything that jumps out to you and is related to your goals.

It is also a great idea to do a targeted search on the internet to find all relevant visual stimuli for representing your goals.

So here are some examples: Let's say you want a vacation in Ireland, then you can cut out pictures of beautiful places in Ireland, then you can cut out pictures of beautiful places in Ireland, airline vouchers for a two-way flight to Ireland, invoices from your favorite Irish vacation rental, etc. Let your imagination run wild, sky is the limit here!

Create your collage

Time to glue or tape all your gathered material in a visually appealing way on your poster board!

Hanging Your Vision Board

Your Vision Board must be hung in a place where you spend a lot of time. Like; the wall in front of your chair while you sit in your office, or your bedroom wall, etc. It is understandable that you might be feeling a bit uncomfortable about hanging something so personal at a place where others can also see it, but you can always just pretend that it is a piece of wall décor. And, indeed, it is by all means an excellent wall décor!

People might get a bit suspicious though when all that your "wall décor" represents begins to come true in your life, but then who cares! (chuckle) What matters is that you will be living your dreams, everything else is inconsequential.

Final Words

Let your imagination run wild while you create your vision board. Nothing is carved in stone here, use your creativity and follow your heart to create something that has genuine emotional appeal to you. Also, even if you are not totally happy with everything you have gotten in place by now, or you find a new piece of magazine cut-out that resonates better with your goals, you can always go back and make modifications.

The whole idea is that the more completely engrossed you are in the process of creating your desired Reality, the sooner it is all going to happen. Having a Vision Board in front of you also makes it easier to eliminate distracting thoughts while keeping your mind focused on what you want.

Therefore, keep your eyes glued to your Vision Board as long as you can every day. For instance, you might be on a client call in your office striking a business deal but your eyes are set firmly on the materialization of your most deeply cherished career dreams. Each time you look at your Vision Board, smile and let a rush of excitement and joy fill your heart because your desires are indeed rapidly manifesting!

Even when you are not physically in the presence of your Vision Board, you can still hold its vision inside your mind. Every time your mind strays or becomes full of doubts, gently bring it back to your dream vision. Also, don't think that you have to stop with just one Vision Board. You can make as many as you like and it might even be a good idea to help your loved ones make their very own Vision Boards. It could be your next fun DIY project with your child or your partner!

Never forget, you have infinite power inside you to create the life you want. When you send out a clear intention of exactly what you want, the universe has to swirl and twirl in your favor!

Action Strategy

1. What you see is what you get so always hold a clear image of what you want.

2. Create your very own Vision Board by letting loose your creativity and imagination.

3. Hang your Vision Board at a place where you spend maximum time.

4. Hold the image of your vision board inside your mind at all times. Feel positive emotions that you are already living everything that your Vision Board represents.

Affirmation

"At this very moment, all that I want is already mine.
As I rejoice in the glory of success, boundless happiness fills
my heart and gratitude floods my being.
I am indeed a child of the Infinite Universe."

Notes

_____

_____

_____

_____

_____

_____

_____

_____

_____

_____

_____

_____

_____

_____

_____

_____

_____

_____

Notes

Chapter 7
Meditation and Manifestation

"Never surrender your hopes and dreams to the fateful limitations others have placed on their own lives. The vision of your true destiny does not reside within the blinkered outlook of the naysayers and the doom prophets. Judge not by their words, but accept advice based on the evidence of actual results.

Do not be surprised should you find a complete absence of anything mystical or miraculous in the manifested reality of those who are so eager to advise you.

Friends and family who suffer the lack of abundance, joy, love, fulfillment and prosperity in their own lives really have no business imposing their self-limiting beliefs on your reality experience."
— *Anthon St. Maarten*

Meditation is the process of connecting with your 'true Self.' Your true Self is the real you – the YOU who is beyond limitations of time and space with the potential to manifest every desire into physical reality.

When you sit still in meditation and connect with your true Self, you reclaim your ability to create the reality of your choice. In meditation your mind becomes like a pond in which the waters are still so that the reflection of the glorious moon of supreme consciousness can be reflected in it.

If you will take some time out in your day for meditation, then trust me you will accelerate the manifestation process of your dreams by leaps and bounds!

When Should You Meditate?

The absolute best time to meditate is immediately before going to bed and immediately upon waking up. This is because easiest to access and reprogram the subconscious during these two times. As we have discussed earlier, your subconscious is the true creator of your reality and reprogramming the subconscious is of paramount importance for manifesting your desires.

In addition to these two important times of the day, you can meditate at any other time also. But I would suggest that you meditate at least during one of these two times. Let all other times of the day be an addition to this basic practice.

If you have never meditated before, then you can start off with as little as 5 minutes and then gradually build up the practice to about half an hour. Advance meditators can even meditate up to an hour or longer, but that is not required for this kind of a manifestation meditation. However, you can do your practice for as long as you want as per your desires.

Be sure to start off with smaller goals as persistence is the key for success.

Where Should You Meditate?

Choose a quite stop where you will not be disturbed by anyone. Try to be away from distractions like cell phones, computers, doorbells, etc. If you want then you can make the ambience even more relaxing by lighting incense and candles. You can also play some soft soothing music in the background.

The Meditation Posture

It is advisable to sit cross-legged with your spine as straight as possible. If this is too difficult then you can also sit on a chair. Just make sure that your back is straight at all times. You can also lie on the bed and do this meditation, but it is not the best thing to do as you will be more likely to dose off while lying in bed.

Meditation for Manifestation Technique

Take deep breaths to completely relax body and mind. Focus all your concentration on your breath – notice how you are taking each breath in, notice how you are exhaling each breath out. Continue doing this until you feel fully relaxed.

Now, imagine yourself in a beautiful garden with lovely flowers and tall trees all around. It's a gorgeous sunny day and all the colors are bright and vibrant. Walk around and bask in the glorious beauty of your surroundings.

There's a long bridge in the middle of the garden. Walk up to the bridge. You can't see the end of this bridge, but you know that on the other side lie all your dreams. With happiness and joyful anticipation of what lies on the other side, begin slowly walking across the bridge.

As you are getting closer and closer to the end of the bridge, you can see all your dreams manifested in physical reality in front of your eyes. Walk into this beautiful picture and become one with your dreams. Let your soul soar high with the joy of fulfillment and let your heart fill with unparalleled happiness.

At this moment, you are grateful to have everything you had ever wished for. Your body is pulsating with an overwhelming sense of happiness and your soul is filled with gratitude. You are so happy and so very grateful to have all your desires fulfilled.

Now, notice a golden light descending from high up above and surrounding everything around you, including your entire being. Your heart is beating with unconditional love and the love from your heart is seeping into everything that surrounds you inside the golden light. At this moment, know that everything you have wished for is already yours. "My every wish is fulfilled. Everything comes to me in perfect Divine Timing."

Slowly step back towards the bridge and walk back into your present. Gently move your toes and fingers, rub your palms together and place them on your eyes. Slowly and lovingly, open your eyes.

Trust that the reality you just experienced is already part of your present reality and should soon be right in front of you. In the meanwhile, fill your heart with happiness, love and gratitude for having received everything you wanted!

You can record this meditation in your own voice and play it back to you while meditating, if desired.

Affirmation
"As my mind calms down, my body relaxes and my worries ease.
I know that I am the architect of my destiny and, at this moment, I am choosing to reclaim my power."

Notes

Notes

_____

_____

_____

_____

_____

_____

_____

_____

_____

_____

_____

_____

_____

_____

_____

_____

_____

_____

_____

Chapter 8
Mastering the Art of Manifestation
– A Quick Recap

"What you think and what you feel and what actually manifests is ALWAYS a match – no exception." – Esther Hicks

Manifestation is a science based on laws that work every single time. So let's evaluate all the components of the formula through which we can manifest anything and everything!

The Power of Thoughts

Never forget that at this very moment you are creating your future and influencing your present with the thoughts inside your mind. The equation is very simple.

Positive thoughts = Positive circumstances + positive people. Negative thoughts = Negative circumstances + negative people.

The choice is yours and the moment of power is in the NOW!!

Emotions Add Fuel to the Fire

Thoughts become powerful because of the emotions behind them. When you think you are a loser, this isn't just a thought inside your head. There is a definite emotional reaction you can feel inside your body and mind to the idea of your being a loser. This leaves you feeling drained and jaded with, perhaps, a strange hollowness in your heart.

On the other hand, when you are thinking about how wonderful your life is, you feel elated and happy. There is a spring in your step and your heart feels like it is soaring high.

So here, you must remember that each thought that crosses your mind comes accompanied by certain emotions. When you think negative, you feel awful and sick. On the other hand, when you think thoughts of happiness and gratitude, you feel an overwhelming sense of wellbeing and joy.

All this is because of the science of energy. Negative thoughts that come accompanied by negative emotions vibrate at a very low frequency. When we resort to negative thinking, we allow ourselves to vibrate at a very low frequency. This in turn, attracts experiences and people of equally low frequency.

So if you want to attract wonderful positive people and circumstances into your life, then you must choose the thoughts you think and the feelings you feel along with them very carefully.

It is easy to predict the future; what you are feeling right now is most likely what you are going to be feeling in the future as well. Therefore, choose to feel happy and elated right now and your future will immediately transform into a happy and joyful one!

Define Your Goals and Set Your Standards High

Knowing what you want is the most important step for manifesting what you want. You can't manifest what you don't know you want!

Once you know what your goal is then you must write it down and promise yourself that you are going to achieve it and that it is indeed doable. Don't let any inhibitions or doubts arise; trust that the Universe is not bound by any limitations. No matter how wild your dreams may be, they will definitely manifest as long as you remain consistent in your approach.

Don't compromise, don't settle for less than what you know you deserve because there is indeed plenty in the Universe for everyone and each wish is guaranteed to be fulfilled as long as we have faith in the infinite Universe.

So take your first step in faith by writing down your goals and know that it has already been granted to you!

Hold on Tight to Your Vision

Visualize what you want as often as you can. You must make your dreams a part of your current reality by holding the vision of their having come true right at this moment inside your mind's eye.

Lights, Camera Action!!

You are the director of your own life. Once you have written down your goals, you must create a practical action plan to achieve your goals. Act on your goals every day with persistence and the movie of your life will turn out exactly how you want it to be. You are the director and you have the power to make it what you want it to be!

The Importance of Persistence

Sometimes people don't get what they want simply because they gave up too easily. Don't give up on your goals until they materialize because they definitely are going to turn into reality sooner or later. Keep walking and don't stop until you have reached your destination.

The Infinite Universe's Proven Manifestation Formula

Thoughts + Emotions + Goal + Visualization + Action + Persistence = YOUR DREAMS TURN INTO REALITY!!

Affirmation

"Right at this moment, all my dreams are turning into reality.
Everything best that the Universe has to offer finds its way to me.
I am blessed with health, wealth, happiness and everything good."

Notes

Notes

Chapter 9
Manifestation and Miracles – An Inspiring Story

On a cold winter night, the kind when the world seems like a dreary and gloomy place, Damien Rodriguez sat on the wooden floor of his freezing cold drafty house. Huddled in a corner next to the barren fireplace, he had his face buried in his palms, totally unaware of the temperature of the room or even of his hands and feet that had been like blocks of ice for a while. He could feel nothing except for a sense of glaring emptiness – so profound that it left him numb towards all other physical sensations.

Damien's life had fallen apart, and, on this day, the final straw that had so far held it tenuously together broke – his wife left him. It felt as if there was no reason to live anymore, but even if he wanted to live he did not know how he could go on living.

The past one month had been a very difficult one – Damien lost his job due to cost-cutting layoffs at work, his wife had undergone an abortion due to which they had fallen apart even more and about two weeks ago, he had discovered that he owes his bank three thousand dollars in credit card debt.

Despite his qualifications and experience, Damien had been finding it increasingly difficult to secure a job. Somehow even when he would be the most highly qualified and experience person showing up for an interview, someone else will end up grabbing the position. Damien had begun to feel completely dejected and was constantly questioning his sense of self. It didn't help that his wife was also going through an intensely difficult period emotionally after the loss of their child.

She craved comfort and security, but he was so jaded emotionally that he could barely help her. This had created a startlingly wide communication gap between them. It seemed like they barely talked anymore and were living like strangers in the same house. They were both clearly fighting their own individual battles and did not have the strength to deal with that of the other's.

Today, when the mailman came in with a book she had long ago ordered online on pregnancy and baby care, Damien simply received the package and left it on the dining table for her. When she came in the kitchen, Damien was sitting on his computer applying to new jobs. She picked up the brown colored package with her name on it and unwrapped it. What she saw left her hysterical in a feat of tears. There was yelling and screaming so intense that Damien felt it would tear his heart apart.

Damien, shocked to the core and not knowing what to do, stepped next to her trying to comfort her. She was crying and yelling, "Why me, why, why did God take away my baby, why, why, why???"

Until this point Damien and his wife, Rosa, had never had a conversation about the whole thing. She was waiting for him to come to her, comfort her and talk about it, but not knowing how to express his emotions he kept to himself.

The fact that he had so many other things on his platter to deal with made it even worse.

In this moment, he was caught totally off-guard, not knowing what to say, what to do, he just managed to get a few half-choked words out, "He is gone, let's just accept it."

These few words acted like a bolt of lightning on his wife, she jerked him off her and in a violent fit of anger told him, "Back off, fuckin' jerk." She stomped her foot like a mad lioness and turned her eyes away from him in rage, determined in that moment of passion to finally take the step she had been contemplating for a while.

Damien had no idea what he had done so awfully wrong. All he wanted to do was comfort her and all this time he avoided talking about it because he thought that talking about it will make it even more difficult for both of them to put this sad memory behind them. He sat there on the dining table chair, shaken and totally frozen. He didn't know how much time passed, but after probably about an hour, his wife came downstairs to the kitchen with two large suitcases and said just three fateful words, "I am leaving."

Damien felt like he had been stabbed in the heart and he ran after her like a desperate school kid, pleading and begging her not to leave. He would do everything he possibly could to fix everything, he just needed another chance. But his wife knew that enough was enough. She just couldn't take it anymore. She finally loaded all her stuff in the car, got on the front seat, told him to back off the car and speedily drove away.

Damien stood there staring at his wife's car even long after it had disappeared from view. He felt as if the ground beneath his feet had been swept away. With a heart as as heavy as led, barely able to hold his body weight together, he walked inside the house and crashed right next to the barren fireplace on the wooden floor of the living room.

Since that moment he had been sitting at the exact same spot – too numb to react, too distraught to hope, too dead to believe he was still alive.

The world just faded away from his view and he did not know where he was. Suddenly a figure appeared in front of him. He said, "Hello Damien!" Totally sure that he was hallucinating, Damien pinched himself. The figure just laughed, "I am for real, you know that."

As scared as Damien was, he managed to say, "Who are you? What do you want? How did you get inside my house?" The figure who looked exactly like him except perhaps more like his younger self from a few years ago said, "Damien, I have always been here. I am your inner Self – your consciousness. You have ignored me for so long, but I was always around. You have been choking my voice and my advice. No wonder you have created such a disaster for yourself and now you are sitting there and mourning at the miseries you have created for yourself."

Damien said, "What do you mean? I haven't created all this? Why will I want to go through all this?"

His Inner Self said, "Tell me, hadn't you been thinking

constantly that you would most likely lose your job ever since you heard about the recession and layoffs? Were you also not thinking what will you do if you lost your job and there were unpaid bills to pay? Were you not losing sleep at night wondering how you would afford your wife's and baby's medical costs? Hasn't the idea of a baby coming into this world felt very scary to you lately? Did you not wish that perhaps this isn't the right time for you to be a father?"

Damien knew it was all very true, but at the same time it was all so hard to accept that he said angrily, "Are you saying that I caused the abortion of my child?!!"

Inner Self, "Well, maybe, not intentionally but ignorantly you did."

Damien said, "Who are you to blame me for murdering my own child?"
Inner self with a roaring laughter, "Ha ha, I am your own inner voice. If you are hearing what you are hearing right now, it is because you carry intense feelings of guilt and self-hatred towards your own self with respect to everything that has come to pass. You think you don't deserve anything good and are not capable of making anything good happen."

Damien just sat there quietly, not knowing what to say because he knew that every word he was hearing was truth to the letter.

Finally, after several minutes he muttered sheepishly, "I don't want to be like this."

His Inner Self responded, "Then change it!!"

Damien, "How?"

Inner Self, "Just like you have created this miserable world for yourself, you can create a beautiful one."
Damien, "But how? And what do you mean by I have created all this."

Inner Self, "Damien who we become and how our life turns out is a result of what we think. If you look at your fearful and negative thoughts, then it will make sense why everything is the way it is. Change your thoughts and you can turn your life around."

Unsure and somewhat unconvinced, Damien said, "But how? How can I change everything? I don't even know where to start??"

Inner Self, "Start by defining what you want. What is it that you really want? If you really want to have the job you are interviewing for tomorrow, then don't go for the interview thinking you are definitely going to be rejected like you have been doing for the past one month. Think that you already have the job and you have it on your own terms. Allow yourself to feel happy and grateful to have secured such a wonderful job. Positive happy emotions are the key for manifesting your thoughts and desires in physical reality. If you will go on attaching your emotions to negative thoughts and ideas, then the cycle of manifesting misery and suffering will never end."

Damien, "But it's so hard to change something that seems to not even be in my control."

Inner Self, "That's only because you have allowed your mind and your emotions to dominate you. Claim your power back. You are the master and your mind is your salve."

Damien, "How do I start?"
Inner Self, "I suggest that you write down exactly what all you want."

Damien, "Well, I can tell you right now exactly what I want. I want a job that pays me $100,000, I want my wife to come back, I want to be debt-free and I want my wife to get pregnant again."

Inner Self, "Then let go of all your fears attached to the manifestation of these things. Trust that it has all been given to you and live as if you already have it all."

Damien, "Sounds like I would be make-believing."

Inner Self, "Life is a make-believe. Whatever you believe in becomes your reality. Only thing is that until now you have been doing it ignorantly creating all the things you don't want."

Damien, "I want to have a good life."

Inner Self, "Then you must work on yourself and it all begins with changing yourself and your thought patterns!"

Damien, "How do I start?"

Inner Self, "It's simple, write down exactly what you want and then write down affirmations that you already have all those things. Read them, repeat them in your mind all the time. Feel inside your heart all the nice warm feelings you would be feeling if it was all there in physical reality."

Suddenly Damien felt startled and opened his eyes. There was no one around. He looked at the wall clock hanging next to the fireplace, it was three in the morning. Like a sudden electric shock, the tremendous sense of pain and hollowness came back, but Damien remembered everything he had just witnessed.

Determined to fix his life, he shook away these feelings. Slowly, but with determination, he gathered himself, got up and went upstairs to their bedroom.

He took out the light brown color leather diary with parchment paper that his wife had gifted him last year on Christmas. Opening a fresh page, he began writing down He took out the light brown color leather diary with parchment paper that his wife had gifted him last year on Christmas.

Opening a fresh page, he began writing down everything he wanted as if it had all already happened. Feeling happiness and joy inside his heart, he would momentarily pause the writing to watch the whole thing in 3D inside his mind's eyes. It felt real and not knowing when, Damien fell asleep.

With sunlight falling on his eyes, Damien suddenly opened his eyes. What he saw shocked him – he thought he was dreaming or perhaps hallucinating. Rosa was right in front him, standing there looking at him lovingly with streams of tears flowing down her eyes. Damien had to pinch himself to make sure this was all real. He was afraid that just like his Inner Self, she too will disappear in thin air.

But Rosa stood there, with tearful eyes and a choking heart, she said, "I am sorry. I know you have been going through a lot lately."

Overwhelmed with a surge of emotions, Damien replied, "I am very sorry. I wasn't there for you. I have been so stupid. I am really sorry."

At this moment, Rosa stepped forward and wrapped her arms around him in a tight embrace. Damien was shaken, still finding it too hard to believe that this was happening, but not wanting to miss the moment, he hugged her tightly too.

They talked and talked, sharing all the buried emotions and feelings. Finally, Rosa understood that the loss of their baby had been equally tough for Damien even though his coping response had been different from hers. She knew that he loves her and was only trying to do the best that he could even when he wouldn't be able to say the right things.

She felt a lot of love and warmth inside her heart. Suddenly, looking up at the clock, she said, "Don't you have to go to an important interview today?"

Damien said, "Yes, I have to. I am a little nervous about it." Rosa said, "Please don't be. I am sure you will get this one. You are the best."

And then she kissed him. It was such a beautiful kiss filled with love and reassurance, something Damien hadn't felt in a long time. It worked like magic on him – reviving his collapsed self-esteem and sense of worth.

Enthusiastically he got up, "Okay, I will go take a shower and get ready."

Rosa lovingly smiled, "I will fix something for you for breakfast."

As Damien was getting ready, after putting his best suit and shining shoes on, he looked at himself in the mirror admiring what he saw. He knew he looked great and he felt that. Throughout that morning, he had been replaying in his mind all the conversation he had had with his inner self the previous night and was implementing everything he learned.

While taking the shower and while getting ready, he had kept repeating to himself, "I have an amazing job as a financial consultant with the biggest investment bank in the United States at a salary of $100,000. My work is deeply fulfilling and makes me very happy. I love going to work every day."

He had also been seeing himself sitting at a lovely customized desk in his new office with all his personal memorabilia, especially the picture of his wife and him from their honeymoon in St. Lucia and a customized mug she had gifted him last year on Valentine's day.

Damien was happy and every time fear or doubt creeped in his heart, he gently brought his mind back to the glorious picture of his fulfilled dreams.

Feeling confident and hopeful, Damien ate his breakfast while making chatty conversation with Rosa. She could tell that he was in especially high spirits and that made her feel light and happy too. As he kissed her goodbye, she wished him good luck.

Rosa stayed home preparing the deliveries for her online knitting business. As evening approached, she began to grow a little worried since she hadn't expected Damien to be away for so long. She had prepared a special dinner for him – lasagna with an extra helping of cheese – just the way he liked it!

Suddenly the handle of the main door moved, with a pounding heart, Rosa anxiously awaited the incomer. With his head hanging low, Damien entered. Afraid that things didn't go right, Rosa asked in a low voice, "How did it go?" Damien suddenly burst in giggle and smiles. Swiftly running up to her, he picked her up in his arms, screaming with happiness, "I got the job!!!!!"

p.s After a couple of months the other miracle also happened. Rosa got pregnant again and this time with twins (yes, Damien created this too). Never forget, life is what we choose to believe in, the Universe always – each time and every time - delivers exactly what we ask for!! And oh yeah, what about his debt? Debt; what debt?

Chapter 10
Affirmations for Manifestation

Pick the affirmations that appeal to you the most and practice them as often as you can. Record them in your voice, play them repeatedly on your music system, write them down, chant them inside your head; do whatever you like. The bottom-line is to make them a part of your life and your subconscious as much as you can because this will greatly accelerate the manifestation process!

Good Health

1. I am very grateful to have a beautiful and healthy body.
2. I love my body. My body is in great shape and excellent health.
3. It is easy and natural for me to make healthy choices. I eat wholesome nutritious food and exercise regularly.
4. My body is full of vitality and energy. Each and every organ of my body functions perfectly.
5. Perfect physical, mental and emotional health is my birthright. I am claiming it right now!
6. I like taking good care of my body. I am blessed with perfect good health
7. My body is strong, healthy and fit. My mind is balanced and calm.
8. Every single cell of my body is filled with good health, vitality and wellness.

9. I am grateful to be enjoying vibrant health in my body and mind
10. Every single organ, tissue and cell of my body is overflowing with divine healing energy. I am perfectly healthy and peaceful.

Happiness

1. My life is full of happiness and joy. I am grateful to be enjoying all the best things in life.
2. With gratitude, I am allowing the Universe to pour health, happiness and wealth into my life.
3. I love myself. I am the source of my own happiness.

4. My heart is filled with joy as I am appreciating all the big and small things I am blessed with.

5. No matter what circumstances come up, I am always happy and peaceful.
6. At this moment, I have everything I need for being happy.
7. I am releasing all my fears and doubts. My heart is now filled with unconditional love and faith.
8. I know that I have been born to enjoy all the best things in life.
9. My presence brings a lot of happiness to others.
10. It is easy and natural for me to be constantly thinking happy and cheerful thoughts.

Career

1. I am working at my dream job making $____. I am extremely happy and fulfilled with my work
2. I deserve to be successful in my dream career. With an open heart, I am accepting it right now.
3. I am surrounded by new opportunities. All known and unknown doors of success are opening for me.
4. I love the work I do. It gives me a sense of purpose and meaning.
5. I am presented with the perfect opportunities to expand my career.
6. I love what I am doing and I am doing what I love.
7. As I allow myself to do what I love doing, money and abundance find a way of coming to me.
8. My ideal job is coming to me in perfect divine timing.
9. I am destined to be a huge success in my career.
10. I am divinely guided to make the best career choices.

Work and Workplace

1. I look forward to going to work every day and having another amazing day.
2. I am absolutely brilliant at everything I do. My work is greatly appreciated by everyone.
3. My work gets me excited. I am passionate about what I do.
4. I am surrounded by wonderful positive people at my workplace.

5. I am blessed to have the most amazing boss in the world.
6. I truly enjoy the company of those I work with.
7. Everyone at work respects and appreciates me.
8. My work is deeply satisfying to me. I am enjoying greater happiness and fulfillment in life because of the work I do.
9. I am handsomely rewarded for all the amazing work I do.
10. I am a huge success at my work.

Fulfilling Relationships

1. I am enjoying great happiness and joy through all my relationships
2. I am blessed to always attract nurturing and loving relationships into my life.
3. I am able to communicate effectively and frankly in all my relationships.
4. I am a very understanding and empathetic person.
5. I always make time for the people who matter most.
6. All my personal and professional relationships bring great joy to me.
7. My partner and I share the most extraordinary love two people have ever shared.
8. I am secure and happy in all my partnerships.
9. I feel profound love and gratitude for all the wonderful relationships I have in my life.
10. I am receiving great love and care from all the important people in my life.

Manifesting Your Soulmate

1. My world is filled with happiness and joy as I am spending every day of my life with my soul mate.
2. I know that my soul mate will find a way of coming to me when the time is right.
3. I am peaceful, relaxed and assured that my soul mate is on his/her way.
4. Being head-over-heels in love with my soul mate even before seeing their physical body is the most amazing thing I have ever experienced.
5. I am enjoying my last days of being single. I know that it is destined to change soon.
6. My soul mate meets all my expectations and even exceeds them.
7. I know that it is possible to love and be loved completely and unconditionally.
8. My soul mate is worth waiting for.
9. At this moment, I am choosing to let go of all doubts, fears and insecurities that could be standing between my soul mate and me.
10. I know that the Universe is going to bring my ideal partner to me on the right day and at the right time.

Financial Abundance

1. I am earning the exact amount of money I want to have every month.
2. I am enjoying great prosperity and abundance in every aspect of my life.

3. I deserve to be handsomely compensated for all the wonderful work I do.
4. The best and most rewarding opportunities find a way of coming to me.
5. I am releasing all negative beliefs and blockages. Money is now abundantly and joyously flowing into my life.
6. The Universe always provides me with more than what I need.
7. I have faith that all my financial needs are taken care of. There is no need to worry about anything.
8. I am receiving great wealth from all sources of cosmic abundance.
9. I trust that there is plenty in the Universe for everyone.
10. I am attracting and accepting all the wonderful gifts the Universe is providing me with.

For a More Positive Life

1. Each day of my life is full of wonderful opportunities, loving people and lots of joy.
2. Every morning when I wake up, I look forward to all the amazing things I am going to do.
3. I attract positive loving people into my life who have my best interest at heart.
4. I feel safe and secure. I know that the Universe is looking after all my needs and desires.
5. My life is perfect and awesome in every way.

6. My life is a perfect manifestation of all my deeply cherished dreams.
7. It is easy for me to release the past. I know how to appreciate and live in the present.
8. I am deeply grateful for all the blessings I have.
9. All my actions and words are guided by unconditional love.
10. My world is an incredibly happy and peaceful one. I always see the good in others and in every situation.

Love

1. My heart is overflowing with happiness, joy and unconditional love.
2. It is easy for me to give and receive love.
3. I am releasing all negative blockages. Love is flowing freely in my life now.
4. I love myself. I am enough to fulfill all my emotional needs.
5. Instead of expecting, I believe in giving love.
6. I am graciously accepting all the love that is flowing to me.
7. I am worthy of great love and everything wonderful.
8. The more content I am in my own self-love, the greater is the love I experience through my relationships.
9. People find it easy to love and appreciate me.
10. I know that I am absolutely adorable and lovable.

Positive Self-Image

1. I am the best ME I can ever be.
2. Everything about me is perfect. I am deserving of nothing but love and appreciation.
3. I like spending time and money on myself. I know I deserve it
4. My body is an incredibly beautiful temple for my soul. I love my body.
5. I am perfectly lovable exactly the way I am.
6. My presence and my smiles brighten the hearts of everyone who crosses my path.
7. By being exactly who I am, I am a blessing to this world.
8. Every part of my body is perfect and beautiful just the way it is.
9. No matter what happens in life, I always have faith in myself.
10. I am destined for greatness and I know that inside my heart.

Bonus Chapter
Discovering your Purpose

"To be successful, the first thing to do is fall in love with your work." – Sister Mary Lauretta

Do you sit in the car and simply head in any direction without knowing exactly where you are going? Obviously not! Then, how can you expect to arrive at massive success and enormous happiness without knowing exactly which road to take to get there?

To tell you a little secret: the road that leads there is mapped out by knowing exactly what your life purpose is! Without knowing exactly what excites you as an individual, work and pretty much everything else in life will continue to feel like a drag. You will continue to do what everyone else is doing simply because that is what people do.

Or it could be that you grew up in a working-class home where you watched your parents dutifully put in their shifts at "the plant." They worked Monday through Friday from 7 am to 4 pm, just so they could enjoy the weekend off and have two weeks at the campground each summer.

So now, caught up in the same pattern, you find yourself working while impatiently waiting to get out of the office. You work just so that you can pay your bills and have some time to yourself.

Or maybe, you went to college and studied law or sales or biology, and now you feel trapped in a job you don't love. You'd like to change course, but then there's this nagging fear of what IF you make the wrong choice? Then there are these other doubts: What else are you even qualified to do? What about the student loan?

The truth is, there are millions of people out there who trudge off to work every day, wishing they were anywhere but at work. They hope in vain and in partial disbelief to one day to find what really inspires them.

If that's you, then rest assured, you are not alone!

An Alternate Scenario

Now imagine, waking up every single morning looking forward to having another amazing day at work?

Imagine... looking forward to Monday mornings as if it was the best day of the week.

Imagine... being one of those people who love their work so much that it doesn't seem like "work" at all.

Imagine... being so passionately in love with your work that working becomes such a fun and rewarding experience that you lose all track of time while doing it.

You must be wondering right now: All that sounds good, but only a few lucky ones have something like that in their life. Well, trust me, you too can have it! Getting there is a process and a journey. Together, through this workbook, we will chart out our path to get there.

Now, I want you to understand that there could be two scenarios. You might get magical results with moments of epiphany in which you will know exactly what you came into this world to do and how to go about it. Or, maybe, it will sow a seed of direction and purpose. Over time, one step at a time, you will get closer to the life of your dreams. The latter scenario might seem like a slower one, but it is by no means inferior.

In the end, no matter which path comes to you naturally, remember that persistence is the key here. Even if you are taking small steps, as long as you are walking in the right direction, you will definitely get to your goal one day. Trust me on this!

So without wasting any time, let's get started!!

Step 1 - Finding Your Interests and Passions

"Trust not what inspires other members of society to choose a career. Trust what inspires you." – The Lazy Person's Guide to Success

Discovering your purpose is all about knowing yourself. You can't know what works best for you without knowing who you are, what you like, what you dislike, what excites you, what turns you off, what you believe in and what you don't believe in.

So set aside an hour or so of uninterrupted time. Head out to the park or a coffee shop. Take this workbook, your favorite notebook and pens with you. Find a quiet corner, and just let your mind wander. Allow your imagination to run wild and don't be afraid to indulge in a lot of unbridled daydreaming.

Imagine... money is not a concern and you have enough dough to manage your day-to-day needs. There is ample left over for fun and entertainment. You now have the freedom to do anything you like with your days.

In your notebook, make a list of all the things you would do with your time if you could spend it any way you liked.

Would you shop?

Would you paint in glorious watercolors?

Would you go back to college and earn a degree in computer science?

Would you travel the world?

Will you be rescuing abandoned animals?

Would you work with abused men and women?

Would you plant a garden or start a florist business?

Just think about exactly whatever it is that comes to you naturally and brings a smile to your face.

What are the things you like doing so much that you lose track of time and appetite while engaged in them?

Don't let your mind interfere by suggesting you can't

possibly make money doing this or that. Remember, right now everything is possible. You are simply allowing yourself to imagine and to get to know yourself better.

If there is even one thing, you are passionate about, it is absolutely possible to make a thriving career out of it even if no one before you has done so. But anyway, for now, let us just focus on your ideal life. If you could spend every day doing whatever you wish with no monetary constraints or obligations, what will you do?

If you get stuck, think about what you do on weekends and holidays. Nearly everyone looks forward to relaxing and enjoying their favorite activities after the workweek is done. What are the activities you most enjoy doing?

Don't forget that the purpose of this exercise is not to make a realistic list of business opportunities, but rather to make a list of possibilities, so don't censor yourself.

Write down whatever pops into your head without considering whether you can make money with it or not, whether you'll love it forever or not, or even whether you have the skills or talent for it or not.

Brainstorming is all about UNFILTERED IDEAS. We will do the filtration later on. For now, just enjoy some daydreaming!

Use the space below and write everything down. If you begin running out of space, use your favorite notebook to pen down your ideas.

Step 2: Start a Journal

"I believe you are your work. Don't trade the stuff of your life, time, for nothing more than dollars. That's a rotten bargain." – Rita Mae Brown

Maybe you already do this, but I want you to challenge yourself for the next 30 days to consistently maintain a daily, purposeful journal. Here's how I recommend doing it.

Fix A Time

First, set aside a fixed time each day for journaling. While any time can be a good time for journaling, for this particular workbook, I suggest doing it as the very last thing in your day. This will help you analyze and review your day to develop a better perspective about yourself and your own life.

Also, the reason why I recommend doing it at a fixed time every day is because that creates a habit and it is harder to break a habit and, therefore, less likely that you will skip your daily journaling.

Let this set time be an unbreakable appointment with yourself. Make yourself do it even on days when it feels hard or uncomfortable. I can guarantee you that pushing yourself harder and disciplining yourself for this step will ultimately turn out to be very rewarding for you!

What to Write

Next, rather than just penning random thoughts and events,

try answering specific questions each day. This type of journaling helps you maintain focus, and it will also allow you to look back later and know exactly what works and what doesn't so that you would have a better idea of where to focus your energy.

Some questions to ask each day include:

1. What was the best thing that happened to me today?

2. How am I feeling right now?

3. What is it that I could have done better?

4. What is it that I want to do tomorrow?

5. What was the most important thing I learned today?

6. How were my relationships with other people today?

7. Was my day efficient?

8. What was the one big thing I got done today?

9. What's one thing I did today just for me?

10. Who made me smile today?

11. What has been my biggest achievement this week?

12. With everything that I have learned today, what are the things I want to do better tomorrow?

There might be other questions you want to add or eliminate. You don't have to stick to the above list completely, just use it for guidance.

Most importantly, enjoy your journaling time! Use it as a means of reflection and also as a source of inspiration. Look forward to what you hope to achieve and take some time every day to reflect on how far you have come. This is an excellent way of motivating yourself.

Every now and then, take the time to read your past writings. Taking note of recurring themes in your journal can be a powerful and effective way of discovering your true passion. You don't know exactly what you might find out about yourself. If the best thing that happens to you every day is the time you serve a delicious dinner cooked with lots of love to your family, then it's clear that being a mom and a great cook are two of your passions. On the other hand, if your day could have been better had it not involved struggling with that annoying accounting software, then clearly bookkeeping is not something you want to pursue.

Another thing to include in your journal is gratitude. No matter how sad or hopeless you might think your day has been, there is always a silver lining – always something to be grateful for! It could be something as small and yet crucial as the fact that the rain didn't start until after your son's last baseball game of the season. Or, maybe, you remembered to take your new sweater out of the dryer and avoided disaster at the last minute.

And if there is nothing else you can think of, it is worth being grateful for the fact that you have a roof over your head, food to eat and clothes to keep you warm.

By writing down the small (and big) things you're grateful for, you will be able to develop and retain a more attitude positive. You will be happier and when you're happy, you're more open to discovering your life's passions.

Also, gratitude sets the Law of Attraction into motion, bringing to you more of all the wonderful things you are grateful for. Remember, whatever it is that you think about and feel most often for manifests in your physical reality.

One last point about journaling—embrace your creative side and do it in a way that feels good to you. Do you feel comfortable typing your words in a word document or does it feel nicer to have a beautiful diary and use an actual pen to write?

You can make the task as aesthetically and creatively appealing as you like. Buy pens in different colors, fill your journal with not just words, but pictures and doodles and anything else that makes you happy. Collect fun stickers to add to your pages, use sticky notes for important points, and feel free to add a photo or two to preserve memories.

Even if you are journaling in a Word document, consider using different fonts, colors and page layouts. Insert pictures and emoticons if you feel like. The idea is to make this as enjoyable as possible so that you look forward to doing it every day rather than it being just another thing you must do!

Exercise: My Daily Journal Questions

In the space below, write down the questions you'll like to ask yourself in your journal. You can take the ones from the list above and write below whatever other questions seem important to you.

Step 3 - Create a Journaling Bag and Space

"Journal writing is a voyage to the interior."

– Christina Baldwin

This step is by no means mandatory, but it might just add more fun to your journaling time in case you decide to implement it. We all know that the right kind of environment can positively influence the work we are doing so having an inspiring and positively reinforcing journaling space might add some fun to your daily writing experience.

So here are some ideas: Set aside a table and a chair for your daily journaling. You can hang a board with inspiring pictures and quotes on the wall above it. You can perhaps also arrange a beautiful lamp with soothing light that relaxes you while writing. And if you want to do your journaling in more style then it might be a good idea to get an old-world ink pot and fountain pen.

Here are some suggestions for supplies that you might want to have around while journaling. Whenever you are traveling, you can tuck them inside a beautiful bag to be able to create the right environment for journaling no matter where you are:

1. Brightly colored pens
2. Sticky notes
3. Colorful Pencils
4. Stamps and stickers
5. Fun-looking Erasers

You might want to write below all the things that you would like to include in your journaling space. Again this isn't mandatory but recommended:

Step 4 - What Are You Sought Out For?

"I have no special talent. I am only passionately curious."
- Albert Einstein

When it comes to finding your true purpose and passion, what others think might seem like the last thing you would want to consider. But the truth is that knowing what others think of when they think of you can offer valuable insight into identifying your own unique genius!

So think about the questions your friends, family, colleagues and even acquaintances come to you for. Do they come to you for assistance with their family finances? Or do you often find yourself hearing about people's problems and offering words of wisdom in return? Do they come to you to get their resume reviewed? Do people solicit your advice in organizing their kitchen? Do you get called upon for career advice? What is it that people most often ask you about?

Whatever it is your friends and family rely on you for, I can tell you that they aren't doing it merely out of loyalty or because they don't want you to feel left out. They do it because they value your input and opinion in certain matters. Knowing exactly what that "matter" is could serve as a guiding light to discovering your natural talents and unique passions.

Do You Have a Superpower?

Ask others if they think you have a superpower. Everyone has at least one, and when you discover yours, you'll very often find it's closely related to your passion.
Superpowers can be anything. Maybe you're a good connector of people or have a knack for creating beautifully written invitation cards. Perhaps you're amazing at creating healthy meals even confirmed junk-food addicts love. Maybe you're simply a great listener to whom helping others selflessly comes naturally.

Step 5 – Simulated Hindsight

"There is nothing noble in being superior to your fellow man; true nobility is being superior to your former self." —
Ernest Hemingway

There's a viral video circulating on the internet of a couple who with the work of a talented team of makeup artists are made to look decades older than they actually are. As they "age" from 30 to 40 to 50 and beyond, they get a glimpse of each other as they might look like in the future. Therefore, for a brief moment, they get to experience what it might be like to grow old together, and what their life might be like decades from the present.

You don't have to do anything that dramatic but simply imagine yourself at 90 years old, looking back at the life you've lived. Your heart is flooded with memories and your home is filled with mementos of the past. There are photos on the walls of your house, your shelves are also filled with trinkets and souvenirs. Inside your heart, you know that it has been a life genuinely well lived.

Think and dream often of exactly what that life looks like!

Step 6 - Write Your Autobiography As You Would Like Your Life To Be

"Writing is the only way I have to explain my own life to myself." — Pat Conroy

Now, here's how you can have some serious fun! Write about your life from the perspective of your older self. Don't worry about your creative writing ability, and don't fret too much over spelling and grammar. This is just for you and you are the only person who is going to be reading it (unless, of course, you want to share it with someone else as well).

So anyway, just spend some time imagining how you'd like to feel at an old age reflecting back on the glorious life you have lived.

Here are some interesting questions to consider while penning the story of your life:

What were the events that made you feel powerful and gave you the greatest sense of accomplishment?

Did you do anything that changed someone else's life for the better?

Who did you have a positive impact on? How?

What was your favorite year? What happened?

What is the most important lesson your children say they learned from you?

What are the best moments and the fondest memories of your life?

Who were the most important people on your journey?

What has been the most important thing for you?

What made your life truly worthwhile?

Step 7 – Enrich Your Life

"No matter who you are, no matter what you did, no matter where you've come from, you can always change, become a better version of yourself." — Madonna

In "The Artist's Way," author Julia Cameron reminds us that creativity cannot survive in a vacuum. She recommends writers and artists spend time in nature and indulge in cultural activities like visiting museums. These activities "refill the well."

This recommendation holds true for all of us because inside we all have a creative Giant just waiting to be awakened. When we manage to awaken this giant, we also get closer to identifying our true purpose in life.

So step out of your house and the four walls of your office to experience something new!

This is the time to try out all those things you've thought you might enjoy but never got round to doing.

So what is it you want to do?

Is it:

Taking a yoga class?

Training for a marathon?

Learning how to design shoes or jewelry?

Signing up for a creative writing course?

Studying for the GMAT?

Riding the Ferris Wheel?

What is it that you have been putting off doing for long?

Only by trying out a variety of activities will you find those that bring you real joy!

Exercise: Plan for New Experiences

Write down everything you would like to experience. This can be a living document that you continue adding on to as new ideas come to you. It's also the document you'll refer to as new opportunities present themselves.

But don't just list things. Make a plan and do them. Add at least one new experience to your calendar every month, then do what it takes to turn it into reality. You might just discover a favorite new hobby while sitting on the Ferris Wheel, or meet your new business partner in the yoga class. Even if nothing that dramatic happens, at the very least, you'll be refilling your own well.

Step 8 - Create an Idea Folder

"Make no little plans; they have no magic to stir men's blood . . . Make big plans; aim high in hope and work." – Daniel Burnham

We all get ideas from time to time. It could be anything from the idea of starting your own healthy meal business to opening a bed & breakfast.

Make it a point to write down every single time the idea of what you CAN DO crosses your mind. If you don't have your folder handy, just make a note in your phone or in a notepad to later scribble it down in your idea folder.

Visit your folder every month to review all the ideas you got in that month. Does anything still sound like a great idea? Someday you might just discover that ONE IDEA which will change your life forever!

If you have any ideas popping at the top of your head right now, write them down in the space provided here without wasting any time!

Step 9 – Putting All The Pieces Together

"If you try anything, if you try to lose weight, or to improve yourself, or to love, or to make the world a better place, you have already achieved something wonderful, before you even begin. Forget failure. If things don't work out the way you want, hold your head up high and be proud. And try again. And again. And again!" — Sarah Dessen

Evaluate everything you have done in the previous steps to answer the following questions:

What recurring theme pops up time and again? (Examples of themes might be technology, children, crafts, animals, or fitness.)

How can I spend my days doing more of those activities and less of the stuff I'm not so fond of?

What gives me a sense of satisfaction at the end of the day?

What are the things I want to improve in myself?

What is the work that I genuinely want to do and make a living out of it?

What are the action steps I can take to turn my passion into a vocation?

Final Word

"Success is a journey, not a destination. The doing is often more important than the outcome." - Arthur Ashe

Following each of these steps is a journey in itself. Even if you don't arrive at that Eureka moment anytime soon in which you would know with total clarity exactly what you want to do for the rest of your life, don't be disheartened.

What truly matters is the fact that with each baby step, you are creating a more deeply fulfilling and happier life.

Enjoying the journey without worrying about arriving at a destination is what matters most and once you begin to genuinely enjoy the journey, you won't even realize it when one day suddenly you will realize that you have arrived at your destination!

Notes

Notes

Follow Issachar Bey at:

 Facebook/Temple of Enlightenment

 Twitter/Temple of Enlightenment

 Instagram/Issachar Bey

 You Tube/Issachar Bey

www.Issacharbey.com

Made in the USA
San Bernardino, CA
09 February 2017